Julia Donaldson is the prize-winning author of the world's best-loved children's books, and was the 2011–2013 Children's Laureate. Her picture books include the modern classic *The Gruffalo*, which has sold over 5 million copies worldwide, and *What the Ladybird Heard*.

Julia also writes fiction, including the Princess Mirror-Belle series illustrated by Lydia Monks, as well as poems, plays and songs – and her brilliant live shows are always in demand. Julia and her husband Malcolm divide their time between West Sussex and Edinburgh.

Nick Sharratt is the prize-winning illustrator of many books for children of all ages. Known for his vibrant, witty illustrations, his picture books with Julia Donaldson include *Goat Goes to Playgroup*, *Hippo Has a Hat*, *One Mole Digging a Hole* and *Chocolate Mousse for Greedy Goose*. He has also illustrated the bestselling Lift-the-Flap Fairy Tales for Macmillan. Nick lives in Edinburgh.

Crazy Mayonnaisy Mum

POEMS BY
JULIA DONALDSON

Illustrated by Nick Sharratt

MACMILLAN CHILDREN'S BOOKS

First published 2004 by Macmillan Children's Books

This edition published 2015 by Macmillan Children's Books
an imprint of Pan Macmillan
a division of Macmillan Publishers Limited
20 New Wharf Road, London N1 9RR
Associated companies throughout the world
www.panmacmillan.com

ISBN 978-1-4472-9322-4

1 3 5 7 9 8 6 4 2

A CIP catalogue record for this book is available from the British Library.

Printed and bound by CPI Group (UK) Ltd, Croydon CR0 4YY

For Caroline

Contents

Noisy Garden

If tiger lilies and dandelions growled,
And cowslips mooed, and dog·roses howled,
And snapdragons roared and catmint miaowed,
My garden would be extremely loud.

Walking the Dog

I take off the lead, open the gate
And watch her run a figure of eight,
And a figure of eight, and a figure of eight,
And another figure of eight.

I walk ten yards along the track
While she goes thundering there and back,
And there and back, and there and back,
And another time there and back.

I settle down upon a log
And watch her chase another dog,
And another dog, and another dog,
And another enormous dog.

I saunter slowly round a lake
While she has a swim and a great big shake,
And a swim and a shake, and a swim and a shake,
And a swim and another big shake.

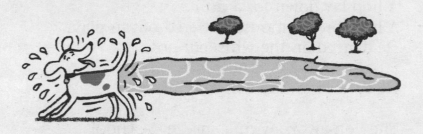

And now those eyes, that look, that lick
Are begging me to throw a stick,
And throw a stick, and throw a stick,
And the stick, and the very same stick.

I've walked a mile and she's run ten.
Back home, I flop while she waits again,
And waits again, and waits again
for the W word again.

The Mouse and the Lion

In the hottest sun of the longest day
A lion lay down for a doze.
A little brown mouse pattered out to play.
He danced on the whiskery nose.
Pit-a-pat, pit-a-pat, pit-a-pat, pit-a-pat,
He danced on the whiskery nose.

The lion awoke with a sneeze, 'A-choo!'
He picked up the mouse in his paw.
'And who may I venture to ask are you?'
He said with a terrible roar.
Grr, grrr, grrrrr, GRRRRRR,
He said with a terrible roar.

'I'll save your life if you'll let me go.'
The mouse's voice shook as he spoke.
The lion laughed loudly, 'Oh ho ho ho.
I'll let you go free for your joke.'
Oho, oho, ohohohoho,
I'll let you go free for your joke.

As chance would have it, the following week
The lion was caught in a net
When all of a sudden he heard a squeak:
'Well met, noble lion, well met.'
Squeak, squeak, squeak, squeak,
Well met, noble lion, well met.

4

The little mouse nibbled and gnawed and bit
Till the lion was finally free.
'It's nothing, dear lion, don't mention it:
I'm repaying your kindness to me.'
Nibbly, nibbly, nibbly, nibble,
Repaying your kindness to me.

'For one of the lessons which mice must learn
From their whiskery father and mother
Is the famous old saying that one good turn
Always deserves another.'
Pit-a-pat, grrr, ohoho, squeak!
Always deserves another.

What's Your Colour?

What's your colour, the colour of your skin,
The colour of the envelope that you're wrapped in?

Is it like chocolate, tea or coffee?
Is it like marzipan, fudge or toffee?
Peaches and cream or a strawberry milkshake
Or does it look more like a curranty cake?

What's your colour, the colour of your skin,
The colour of the envelope that you're wrapped in?

Are you a map of your past disasters?
Grazes and scratches and sticking plasters?
Bites from mosquitoes, a yellow-blue bruise
And a couple of blisters from rather tight shoes?

What's your colour, the colour of your skin,
The colour of the envelope that you're wrapped in?

How does it go when the weather's sunny?
Brown as a berry or gold as honey?
Does it go freckly or peeling and sore?
Is there a mark from the watch that you wore?

What's your colour, the colour of your skin,
The colour of the envelope that you're wrapped in?

Do you go pink when you're all embarrassed?
Sweaty and red when you're hot and harassed?
Bumpy and blue on a cold winter's day?
When it's time for your bath are you usually grey?

What's your colour, the colour of your skin,
The colour of the envelope that you're wrapped in?

Crazy Mayonnaisy Mum

When my friends come home with me
They never want to stay for tea
Because of Mum's peculiar meals
Like strawberries with jellied eels.
You should see her lick her lips
And sprinkle sugar on the chips,
Then pass a cup of tea to you
And ask, 'One salt or two?'

Whoops-a-daisy,
That's my crazy
Mayonnaisy mum.

She serves up ice cream with baked beans,
And golden syrup with sardines,
And curried chocolate mousse on toast,
And once she iced the Sunday roast.
When my birthday comes she'll make
A steak and kidney birthday cake.
There'll be jelly too, of course,
With cheese and onion sauce.

Whoops-a-daisy,
That's my crazy
Mayonnaisy mum.

What's she put in my packed lunch?
A bag of rhubarb crisps to crunch.
Lots of sandwiches as well,
But what is in them? Who can tell?
It tastes like marmalade and ham,
Or maybe fish paste mixed with jam.
What's inside my flask today?
Spinach squash – hooray!

Whoops-a-daisy,
That's my crazy
Mayonnaisy mum.

Name the Day

One two three four five six seven.
Sun and moon and gods in heaven
Worshipped by people down below
Gave the days the names we know.

I'm the sun and my day's Sunday.
I'm the moon, and moon day's Monday.
Brother and sister, round we fly,
Chased by wolves across the sky.

Do I hear you asking whose day
follows Monday? Yes, it's Tiu's day.
Named after me, one-handed Tiu.
Bravest god the Norsemen knew.

I'm Tiu's father, mighty Odin,
Sometimes also known as Woden.
Recently, though, I've heard you say
Wednesday for Woden's day.

Who rules Thursday, you may wonder.
Thursday's Thor's day, god of Thunder.
Fighter of giants, loved and feared,
I breathe blizzards through my beard.

My name's Frig, and Frig's day's my day.
Nowadays you call it Friday.
Queen of the gods and Odin's wife,
I watch over every life.

Just to change the Norse gods' pattern,
I'm a Roman god called Saturn.
I bless the farmers' corn and hay,
And Saturday is Saturn's day.

One two three four five six seven.
Sun and moon and gods in heaven
Worshipped by people down below
Gave the days the names we know.

Cat Envy

The cat is sleeping on my bed.
She's lucky she can sleep, instead
Of lying worrying all night
And wishing she was black and white
Or wondering why the cat next door
Has stopped being friendly any more.

She sometimes gives herself a groom
But no one makes her clean her room,
And no one's going to wake her up
And yell, 'Bring down that empty cup!'
Or, 'If you don't get moving you'll
Be twenty minutes late for school!'

No wonder she can sleep like that.
I sometimes wish I was the cat.

Window Cleaner

If you want a cleaner window
Then you want a window cleaner.
You don't want a butcher or a baker or a banker
Or a bowler or a ballerina.
With my ladder nice and steady
And my wiper at the ready
There is no one who is keener
To give you a cleaner window
Then your very own window cleaner.

Two Wheels

I like to look at photographs of me on my old
   trike.
It had three wheels and never used to wobble
   like my bike.
Three wheels!
Riding on three wheels!
I used to like riding my trike with three wheels.

Stabilisers made my bike easier to ride.
They stopped it falling over when it tilted to
   one side.
Four wheels!
Riding on four wheels!
Not quite a bike, not quite a
   trike, with four wheels.

On the day we took them off, I came off as well,
But now it's great to ride around and tinkle on
  my bell.
Two wheels!
Riding on two wheels!
That's what I like – riding my bike with two
  wheels.

The Wind and the Sun

Said the wind to the sun, 'I can carry off kites
And howl down the chimney on blustery nights.
I can sail boats and set windmills in motion,
Rattle the windows and ruffle the ocean.'

And the old sun grinned
At the wild winter wind.

Said the sun to the wind, 'I turn night into day,
Ice into water and grass into hay.
I can melt puddles and open up roses.
I can paint rainbows, and freckles on noses.'

And the old sun grinned
At the wild winter wind.

Said the wind to the sun, 'You'll be sorry you spoke.
Down on the road is a man with a cloak.
If you're so clever then let's see you prove it.
We'll take it in turns to see who can remove it.'

And the old sun grinned
At the wild winter wind.

The wind blew the trees till the boughs bent and
broke.
He bowled the man's hat off and howled round his
cloak.
He blew and he blustered, he tossed and he tugged it.
The man wrapped it round him and tightly he
hugged it.

16

And the old sun grinned
At the wild winter wind.

'Take a rest,' said the sun. 'Let me shine on him
   now.'
He shone till the man started mopping his brow.
The man settled down in the shade of some
   boulders.
He undid his clock and it slipped from his
   shoulders.

And the old sun grinned
At the wild winter wind.

Roundabout

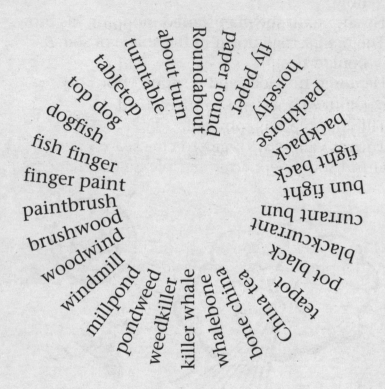

Roundabout
about turn
turntable
tabletop
top dog
dogfish
fish finger
finger paint
paintbrush
brushwood
woodwind
windmill
millpond
pondweed
weedkiller
killer whale
whalebone
bone china
China tea
teapot
Pot black
blackcurrant
currant bun
bun fight
fight back
backpack
packhorse
horsefly
fly paper
paper round
Roundabout

Pizza

Are you ready? Then off you go.
Punch and pummel that pizza dough.
Roll it out with a rolling pin.
Don't stop rolling till it's nice and thin.

Crush tomatoes and gently spread
Till your pizza is ruby red.
Turn it yellow with grated cheese.
Grind some pepper on but please don't sneeze.

Take a knife and begin to slice.
Pepperoni are pretty nice.
Chop some mushrooms and lots of ham.
Add a pinch or two or marjoram.

Now for seafood, and don't be skimpy.
Make your pizza extremely shrimpy.
Add some mussels, and if you wish
A tin of anchovies or tuna fish.

Mamma mia! You've no idea!
It's the finest pizza in the pizzeria!

Two Friends

My friend Lily is little as a pin.
She lives inside a shoebox. She sleeps inside a tin.
When her plates are dirty she takes an acorn cup
And fills it full of raindrops to do the washing up.
She likes to play with greenfly; she keeps one as a
    pet
And she puts it in a nutshell when she takes it to
    the vet.
I wanted Mum to meet her, so I asked her home
    to tea
And she ran about the table playing football with
    a pea.

My friend Trudy is taller than a tower
And once she picked a tree because she thought it
    was a flower
She has skipping ropes for laces on her size-100
    feet,
And when she needs to blow her nose she blows it
    on a sheet.
She takes a lamp-post up to bed to keep away the
    dark
And she says she keeps a tadpole but I'm certain
    it's a shark.
She came to lunch and ate it with a garden fork
    and saw,
Then she snapped a drainpipe off the house and
    used it as a straw.

Questions

How? Who can say how?
How did we travel from Then until Now?
Galaxies hurled and hurtled apart –
How in the world did the whole thing start?
Was there a bang? How long ago?
Does anyone anywhere really know?

Why? Who can say why?
Why did the dinosaur dynasty die?
Why should a beast whose power was colossal
Give up the ghost and turn into a fossil?
Give us a clue; why was it so?
Does anyone anywhere really know?

When? Who can say when?
When did our ancestors turn into men?
Swinging about in the family tree,
When did they start to look something like me?
Heavyweight brain, when did you grow?
Does anyone anywhere really know?

Who? Who can say who?
Who can unravel a riddle or two?
Melting the ice, unwinding the clocks,
Who'll take the lid off the mystery box?
Where do we come from and where do we go?
And who can say who is in charge of the show?
Does anyone anywhere really know?

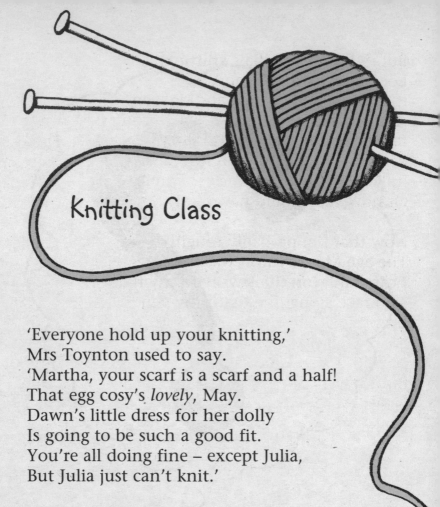

Knitting Class

'Everyone hold up your knitting,'
Mrs Toynton used to say.
'Martha, your scarf is a scarf and a half!
That egg cosy's *lovely*, May.
Dawn's little dress for her dolly
Is going to be such a good fit.
You're all doing fine – except Julia,
But Julia just can't knit.'

Suddenly, one day I got it!
My fingers found out what to do.
Stitch after stitch, row upon row,
My kettle-holder grew.
Mrs Toynton said, 'Hold up your knitting,'
And a fire in my heart was lit.
Today is the day when she's going to say,
'Julia's learnt to knit.'

But: 'All look at Julia's knitting.
Look at it hard and long.
It's ragged and stained and uneven
And she's done all the stitches wrong.
It's loopy and droopy and dirty,
And look at the holes in it!
Julia's knitting's a perfect example
Of how you should never knit.'

Now that I'm probably roughly
The age Mrs Toynton was then,
I can dance on the keys with my fingers
And race along lines with my pen.
I can play the guitar and the piano.
I can even play tennis (a bit),
I mend trousers and skirts, I sew buttons on shirts
But I never
Never
Knit.

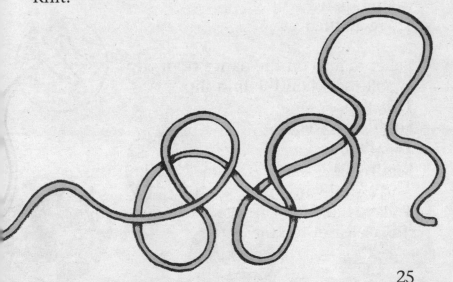

There Go the Feet

Horses' hoofs on the cobbles clatter.
Pigeon toes on the pavement patter.
Clatter, patter,
There go the feet.

High-heeled shoes on the floorboards tap.
Divers' flippers on the wet sand flap.
Tap, flap,
Clatter, patter,
There go the feet.

Bedroom slippers on the staircase shuffle.
Football boots on the playing field scuffle.
Shuffle, scuffle,
Tap, flap,
Clatter, patter,
There go the feet.

Ballet pumps on the dance floor trip.
Woolly socks on the lino slip.
Trip, slip,
Shuffle, scuffle,
Tap, flap,
Clatter, patter,
There go the feet.

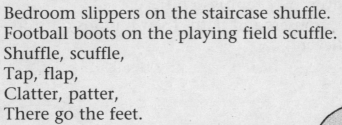

Rabbits' claws in the burrow scrabble.
Children's toes in the water dabble.
Scrabble, dabble,
Trip, slip,
Shuffle, scuffle,
Tap, flap,
Clatter, patter,
There go the feet.

Elephants' feet in the jungle crash.
Wellington boots in the puddles splash.
Crash, splash,
Scrabble, dabble,
Trip, slip,
Shuffle, scuffle,
Tap, flap,
Clatter, patter,
There go the feet.

Size-one shoes in the playpen toddle.
Ducklings' feet round the duck pond waddle.
Toddle, waddle,
Crash, splash,
Scrabble, dabble,
Trip, slip,
Shuffle, scuffle,
Tap, flap,
Clatter, patter,
THERE GO THE FEET!

27

The Tortoise and the Hare

The hare was the handsomest hare in the world
With a white fluffy bobtail and whiskers that
    curled.
He lived in a field and his favourite sport was
Leapfrogging over the back of the tortoise.
The hare went a-loping, a-lolloping, a-leaping.
The tortoise went crawling, a-creaking, a-creeping.

The hare claimed that no one was faster then he.
He asked all the animals, 'Who'll race with me?'
The tortoise said, 'I will!' The hare roared with
    laughter.
'Race with a tortoise? Why, what could be dafter?
I'll go a-loping, a-lolloping, a-leaping.
You'll go a-crawling, a-creaking, a-creeping.'

They mapped out a course and they fixed a day.
It's one two three go! and the hare is away,
Whisking his bobtail and frisking and gambolling.
Way back behind him the tortoise is ambling.
The hare goes a-loping, a-lolloping, a-leaping.
The tortoise comes crawling, a-creaking, a-creeping.

The hare is halfway when he stretches and blinks.
'I've nothing to lose if I snatch forty winks.'
His head drops, his eyes close, and soon he is
    slumbering.
Inching towards him the tortoise is lumbering.
The hare is a-snoring, a-snoozing, a-sleeping.
The tortoise comes crawling, a-creaking, a-creeping.

The hare wakes and starts: is it real or a ghost?
The tortoise is nearing the finishing post.
The hare helter-skelters but just doesn't do it.
Slowcoach the tortoise has beaten him to it.
The hare lost a-snoring, a-snoozing, a-sleeping.
The tortoise won crawling, a-creaking, a-creeping.

On the Pond in the Park

Splash goes the bread. The ripples spread,
Telling the ducks that it's time to be fed
On the pond
In the park.

Green-headed Dad decides to dine.
Brown-speckled Mum leads the kids in a line
On the pond
In the park.

Go away, goose, you're much too greedy.
Leave a few crumbs for the poor and the needy
On the pond
In the park.

Graceful and white, the long-necked swan
Lets out a hiss and the ducks are all gone
From the pond
In the park.

Cheerio ducks and goodbye drakes.
I'm going home to eat biscuits and cakes
Off a plate
In my house.

Buttons

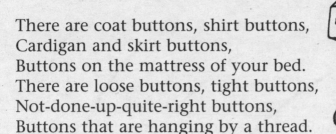

There are coat buttons, shirt buttons,
Cardigan and skirt buttons,
Buttons on the mattress of your bed.
There are loose buttons, tight buttons,
Not-done-up-quite-right buttons,
Buttons that are hanging by a thread.

There are minus and plus buttons,
Let-me-off-the-bus buttons,
Buttons on a fizzy-drinks machine.
There are open-the-door buttons,
Take-me-up-a-floor buttons,
Buttons that can turn the red man green.

There are round buttons, square buttons,
Eyes-on-teddy-bear buttons,
Buttons on a gingerbread man's chest.
But if you're a bit like me
Then I'm sure you will agree
That chocolate buttons are the best.

Santa Claws

I don't know why they're blaming me
When all I did was climb a tree
And bat a shiny silver ball.
How could I know the tree would fall?
And when those silly lights went out
They didn't have to scream and shout
And turf me out and shut the door.
Now no one loves me any more.
I'm in the kitchen by myself.
But wait! What's on that high-up shelf?
A lovely turkey, big and fat!
How nice! They *do* still love their cat.

33

Keeping Warm

I've got a cosy duvet; it keeps me warm enough,
But birds don't need a duvet; they have feathers
   they can fluff.
It helps to keep them warm
In the cold and snow and storm.

When I start to shiver it's nice to have a cuddle,
And maybe that's how birds feel when you see
   them in a huddle.
It helps to keep them warm
In the cold and snow and storm.

When I'm feeling frozen I stamp and run around,
And birds can hop to stop their feet from freezing
   to the ground.
It helps to keep them warm
In the cold and snow and storm.

In the winter weather we turn the heating high,
But some birds fly to hotter lands away across the
   sky.
It helps to keep them warm
In the cold and snow and storm.

Food can keep the cold out. It can be hard to find,
So let's put some of ours out for the birds that stay
   behind
And help to keep them warm
In the cold and snow and storm.

Josephine

Josephine's dad was a juggler.
Her mum was an acrobat.
Josephine's dog was the circus dog.
Her cat was the circus cat.
Josephine's sister tamed the lions.
Her brother swallowed fire.
Josephine's grandma pedalled a bike
Up on the highest wire.
Josephine's friends all came to the show,
But where, oh where was Jo?
Josephine sat in her caravan,
Watching a video.

Animal Orchestra

Hedgehog hums.
Squirrel strums.
Badger bashes on the drums.

Bulldogs blow
High and low.
To and fro goes
bison's bow.

Turtles toot.
Hippos hoot.
Cool koala plays the flute.

Crayfish croons
Catchy tunes.
Crab and lobster play
the spoons.

Tiger thumps.
Carthorse clumps.
Gerbil jumps on camel's
    humps.

Violins
Under chins.
Wagging tails and
    clapping fans.

Swing and sway!
Sing and play!
Stay and dance the night away!

Guinea Pig

I don't need a tin of cat food
Or toad in the hole for my tea,
But grain I can munch and carrots to crunch,
That's the right kind of food for me.

I don't need a tank to swim in.
I don't want a nest in a tree,
But hay in a hutch I'd like very much.
That's the right kind of home for me.

I don't need a field with cows in:
A pen's big enough to feel free,
With grass I can eat right under my feet.
That's the right kind of space for me.

Please don't rub my fur the wrong way:
Just think and I'm sure you'll agree
That hands which can stroke and don't pinch
    and poke
Are the right kind of hands for me.

Luke

Luke liked running round the room.
Luke liked jumping on the bed.
Luke liked splashing in the basin.
What do you think his mother said?

Oh!
Do stop running round the room.
Do stop jumping on the bed.
Do stop splashing in the basin.
Let's go and walk the dog instead.

So
Luke went running round the park.
Luke went jumping off a log.
Luke went splashing in the puddles.
So did his mother and the dog.

The Strongest One

The sun shone down upon a mouse.
The mouse began to squeak:
'I wish I could be strong like you
Instead of small and weak!'

'I may be strong,' the sun replied.
'I may be big and bright,
But one dark rain cloud has the power
To blot out all my light.'

'Oh noble cloud!' the mouse called out.
'Oh high and mighty one!
I'd love to be a cloud like you
And cover up the sun!'

The rain cloud sighed. 'The cold North wind
Is stronger far than I.
I cannot stop him chasing me
Around the stormy sky.'

'Oh powerful wind!' the mouse exclaimed.
'I wish I could be you
And have the strength to drive the rain clouds
Every time I blew!'

The wind replied, 'Beneath your feet
Is something stronger still.
However hard I huff and puff
I can't blow down that hill.'

The mouse, impressed, cried, 'Lofty hill,
How strong and firm you stand!
If only I could be like you,
The ruler of the land!'

The hill then spoke. 'However strong
And solid I may be,
There's somebody more powerful
Who makes holes all over me.'

The mouse was lost in wonder.
Could this strange thing be true?
'Who is this somebody?' he asked.
The hill replied: 'It's you.'

Pondwatch

Then

Our gran was fond
Of coming to the pond
With irises all around.
A dragonfly
Would sometimes catch her eye
And frogs jumped about on the ground.

And there were moorhens, ducks and coots
On the pond.

She used to bring
A jam jar on a string.
She dipped it and pulled it out.
And there were snails
And little things with tails
All crawling and wriggling about

And there were tadpoles, frogs and newts
In the pond.

Now

How could we guess
The pond would be a mess,
A horrible rubbish dump?
No air, no light,
It's like a building site
With no room to wriggle or jump.

And there are bottles, bags and boots
In the pond.

It's time to clear
The cans of ginger beer,
The rubbish and rusty nails,
Scoop off the foam
And make the pond a home
Where tadpoles can twiddle their tails.

Take out the bottles, bags and boots,
Bring back the moorhens, ducks and coots,
Bring back the tadpoles, frogs and newts
To the pond.

Cinderella's Lizard

I was a lizard in the garden, in the wall.
I had no dreams; I was a lizard, that was all

Till Cinderella took me gently from the night
Into a kitchen bright with fire and fairy light

And like a fire the wand-tip touched me, and
   behold –
I was a footman, dressed in purple trimmed with
   gold.

On golden wheels we left the garden and the wall.
White horses drew us to the palace and the ball.

I twirled a kitchen maid around the servants' hall.
Above our heads we heard the music rise and fall.

We strolled around the palace garden, shadows tall.
I laughed aloud to see a lizard on the wall.

The chimes of midnight drowned the music in my
   ear
And when it stopped I saw the carriage disappear.

Some mice, a pumpkin, footsteps running, that was
   all,
And I was scuttle-toed and scaly, green and small.

Before that night I had no dreams, but now I do.
I dream a kitchen maid may one day find my shoe.

I Opened a Book

I opened a book and in I strode.
Now nobody can find me.
I've left my chair, my house, my road,
My town and my world behind me.

I'm wearing the cloak, I've slipped on the ring,
I've swallowed the magic potion.
I've fought with a dragon, dined with a king
And dived in a bottomless ocean.

I opened a book and made some friends.
I shared their tears and laughter
And followed their road with its bumps and bends
To the happily ever after.

I finished my book and out I came.
The cloak can no longer hide me.
My chair and my house are just the same,
But I have a book inside me.

Shuffle and Squelch

Spring brings showers; the world's aflood.
Wellies on, let's brave the mud.
We'll go squelching about, squelching about,
Squelching about in the mud,
Yes we'll go squelching about, squelching
   about,
Squelching about in the mud.

Kick your boots off, everyone.
Summer's here and so's the sun.
We'll go dancing about, dancing about,
Dancing about in the sun,
Yes we'll go dancing about,
   dancing about,
Dancing about in the sun.

Hold your hat; the winds are thieves.
Watch them steal the autumn leaves
As we shuffle about, shuffle about,
Shuffle about in the leaves,
Yes as we shuffle about, shuffle about,
Shuffle about in the leaves.

Wind your scarf round once or twice.
Winter's turned the world to ice.
We'll go sliding about, sliding about,
Sliding about on the ice,
Yes we'll go sliding about, sliding about,
Sliding about on the ice.

Give Us This Day . . .

Oh for the smell of it, out in the street,
Whetting my appetite, guiding my feet
Into the queue for it, there to behold
Rack upon rack of it, brown, white and gold.

Oh for the sound of it – clattering trays
Bringing fresh batches in front of my gaze,
Shiny and seeded or grainy and brown,
A cob and a cottage, a crescent, a crown.

Oh for the feel of it, dusty with flour,
Warm, firm, and ready for me to devour,
My hands to break open, my teeth to embed
In – oh for the taste of it! – wonderful bread.

Cross Katy

Katy didn't want to play,
Not at all, not all day.

'Come on, Katy, let's play tig!'
'No,' said Katy. 'I'm too big.'

'What about a game of ball?'
'No, I don't like that at all.'

'Do you want to climb a tree?'
'You can if you like, not me.'

'Well then, let's play hide and seek.'
'We played that silly game last week.'

'Skipping then? That's good,' I said.
But Katy only shook her head.

So off I went and played with Sue.
Then Katy said, 'Can I play too?'

A Penny for the Guy

A penny for the guy.
A penny for the guy.
Remember me as I used to be.
A penny for the guy.

As I lie here on the pavement, how I wish that
  you could see
Mr Fawkes, the perfect gentleman – the Guy I
  used to be –
Dressed in all the latest fashions, from my shoes
  of Spanish leather
To my wig (complete with ringlets) and my hat
  (complete with feather).
Round my chest I wore a doublet; round my
  neck a golden locket.
A tasselled silken handkerchief protruded from
  my pocket.
My doeskin gloves were perfumed and my ruff
  stood proud and high
And I heard the ladies whispering, 'He's really
  quite a guy.'

A penny for the guy.
A penny for the guy.
Remember me as I used to be.
A penny for the guy.

But now my face is just a mask, with plastic
   nose and lips,
And my body's stuffed with newspaper that
   smells of fish and chips.
I've got two left-foot wellies, which is not the
   thing to wear
When you're creeping round with gunpowder
   upon the cellar stair.
I'd like to hatch a cunning plot to set myself to
   rights
But I can't because my brain consists of laddered
   ladies' tights.
But when I'm on that bonfire and the flames are
   leaping high
I'll hear the ladies whispering, 'He's really quite
   a guy.'

A penny for the guy.
A penny for the guy.
Remember me as I used to be.
A penny for the guy.

The Stork and the Fox

A stork was stretching her legs one day
When a sly old fox came slinking her way.
'Good morning, Stork. I have something to say:
An extra-special request.
I was stirring some soup when I thought of you.
Oh do come and dine with me, Stork, yes do!
Dinner is much better fun with two,
So be my guest.'

When the fox had sounded the dinner gong
The stork found out there was something wrong
For the plate was flat and her beak was long
And not a drop did she taste.
Said the fox, 'You're slimming, it's plain to see,
Or you ate too much for your lunch, maybe.
Just take it easy and leave it to me
For I can't stand waste.'

The fox was brushing his tail next day
When the tall white stork came strutting his way.
'Good morning, Fox. I have something to say:
An extra-special request.
Tonight for supper I dearly wish
That you'd come and join me to eat a dish
Of every kind of delicious fish.
Yes, be my guest.'

As the fox sat down to the meal, he thought,
'There may be a catch but I won't be caught,'
But the jug was deep and his tongue was short
And not a scrap did he taste.
Said the stork, 'You've lost your good appetite
So I'm sure you won't mind if I have the last bite
For I seem to remember you told me last night
That you can't stand waste.'

53

Brain Gym

My brain's a gym, where bright ideas
Turn cartwheels in between my ears.
My plans do press-ups, and my thoughts
Jog up and down in lycra shorts.
My worries lift the weights. My hopes
Swing wildly from the ceiling ropes.

Till, all exhausted, down they lie,
And then my dreams appear . . .
    and fly.

Magpie

I'm a mischief-making magpie. I'm the curse of
    every cop.
Just yesterday I broke into a chocolate shop,
But I left behind the liquorice, the toffees and the
    rest,
And I took some silver paper home to my nest.
Home to my nest, home to my nest,
I took some silver paper home to my nest.

I expect you heard the news about the hold-up at
    the bank.
I bet you didn't know the bank had me to thank,
But I left behind the ten-pound notes, the
    hundreds and the rest,
And I took a shiny 5p home to my nest.
Home to my nest, home to my nest,
I took a shiny 5p home to my nest.

It was twelve o'clock on Christmas Eve and shall I
    tell you what?
I followed Father Christmas down a chimney pot,
But I left behind the stockings and the presents
    and the rest,
And I took a piece of tinsel home to
    my nest.
Home to my nest, home to my nest,
I took a piece of tinsel home to
    my nest.

Class Photograph

Everyone's smiling, grinning, beaming,
Even Clare Biggs who was really scheming
How she was going to get revenge
On her ex-best friend, Selina Penge
(front row, third left, with hair in wisps)
For stealing her salt and vinegar crisps.

And Martin Layton-Smith is beaming,
Though he was almost certainly dreaming
Of warlock warriors in dripping caves
Sending mindless orcs to their gruesome graves.
(Next to him, Christopher Jordan's dream
Has something to do with a football team.)

And Ann-Marie Struthers is sort of beaming,
Though a minute ago her eyes were streaming
Because she'd been put in the second back row
And separated from Jennifer Snow.
And Jennifer Snow is beaming too,
Though Miss Bell wouldn't let her go to the loo.

And Miss Bell, yes even Miss Bell is beaming,
Though only just now we'd heard her screaming
At the boy beside her, Robert Black,
Who kept on peeling his eyelids back
And making a silly hooting noise
(Though he said that was one of the other boys).

Eve Rice is doing her best at beaming.
Yes, Eve is reasonably cheerful-seeming,
Though I think she was jealous because Ruth
  Chubb
Had – at last! – let me into their special club.
(In order to join the club, said Ruth,
You had to have lost at least one tooth.)

And look, that's me, and my teeth are gleaming
Around my new gap; yes, I'm *really* beaming.

Mother's Day

I'm making breakfast for my
  mum, the kind she likes the most.
An egg and milky coffee and a round of buttered
  toast.
The egg is boiling nicely. It needs just ten
  seconds more,
Then I'll . . . Brrring, brrring, brrring brrring!
  'Hello, it's Di next door.'

Natter natter natter natter natter natter natter.
Chatter chatter chatter chatter chatter chatter
  chatter.

The egg's had seven minutes but I don't suppose
  it's spoiled.
I know a lot of people who prefer their eggs
  hard-boiled.
The coffee won't take very long. The milk is in
  the pan,
So I'll . . . Brrring, brrring, brrring brrring!
  'Hello, dear, it's your gran.'

Natter natter natter natter natter natter natter.
Chatter chatter chatter chatter chatter chatter
  chatter.

The milk's boiled dry. I'll have to make some
  lemon tea instead,
But I can't find any lemons, so I think I'll toast
  the bread.
The slice is cut, the grill is hot, it won't be long
  until
I can . . . Brrring, brrring, brrring brrring! 'Hello,
  it's Uncle Bill.'

Natter natter natter natter natter natter natter.
Chatter chatter chatter chatter chatter chatter
  chatter.

My turn to make a phone call. I dial the Fire
  Brigade.
'The toast's on fire! Come quickly, please – and
  bring some marmalade.'

Riddles

I am a lift, a shiny lift,
With thin white passengers to shift.
Squeeze them in and send them down.
When they come up they'll be golden brown.

I'm smaller than a mole,
I'm smaller than a mouse,
And I turn inside my hole
When you go into your house.

I'm partly red and partly white.
I have no wings yet I fly through the night.
I fit in a space that's black and tight.
I come to you heavy, I go back light.

Nippers, grippers, legs in the air.
The wind may blow but we don't care.
Nippers, grippers, all in a row.
Squeeze our legs and we'll let go.

I swallow children, women, men.
I roar and roar and ROAR,
Then stop and spit them out again
And swallow up some more.

All the answers can be found in the picture

Coming Downstairs

My dad comes plodding down the stairs: thump,
    thump, thump.
My sister runs down half a flight, then takes a
    flying jump.
Our baby comes down backwards, with a
    slithering kind of crawl.
My brother tripped the other day and had a
    nasty fall.
My mum comes at the gallop. She sounds just
    like a horse.
And if you hear a padding sound, why that's the
    cat of course.
One step at a time is how Granny comes down
    Granny's stairs.
But I don't come downstairs at
    all – I slide down the banisters.

Kitten on the Farm

'I can't catch mice,' said the kitten on the farm.
'I can't catch mice and my tummy feels hollow.'
'Then my advice,' said the duck upon the pond,
'Then my advice for a kitten to follow
Is to quack quack quack outside the farmer's door.
Quack quack quack, then quack a little more.
Quack quack quack; the farmer will be sure
To find some bread for a kitten to swallow.'

'But bread's not nice,' said the kitten on the farm.
'Bread's not nice and my tummy feels hollow.'
'Then my advice,' said the hen inside the pen,
'Then my advice for a kitten to follow
Is to cluck cluck cluck outside the farmer's door.
Cluck cluck cluck, then cluck a little more.
Cluck cluck cluck; the farmer will be sure
To find some corn for a kitten to swallow.'

'But corn's not nice,' said the kitten on the farm.
'Corn's not nice and my tummy feels hollow.'
'Then my advice,' said the horse upon the hay,
'Then my advice for a kitten to follow
Is to neigh neigh neigh outside the farmer's door.
Neigh neigh neigh, then neigh a little more.
Neigh neigh neigh; the farmer will be sure
To find some hay for a kitten to swallow.'

'But hay's not nice,' said the kitten on the farm.
'Hay's not nice and my tummy feels hollow.'
'Then my advice,' said the cat upon the roof,
'Then my advice for a kitten to follow
Is to miaow miaow miaow outside the farmer's
   door.
Miaow miaow miaow, then miaow a little more.
Miaow miaow miaow; the farmer will be sure
To find some milk for a kitten to swallow.'

'Now milk *is* nice,' said the kitten on the farm.
'Milk is nice and my tummy still feels oh so
   terribly dreadfully hollow.
So your advice, fellow cat upon the roof,
Is good advice for a kitten to follow.'
So she miaow miaow miaowed outside the
   farmer's door.
Miaow miaow miaowed, then miaowed a little
   more.
'Miaow miaow miaow!' The farmer heard and saw.
He found some milk for the kitten to swallow.

Purrrrrrrrrr!

Beanstalk Blues

Fee Fi Fo Fum.
I am a giantess, gloomy and glum.
Why did I let the wee rascal come?

Fi Fo Fum Fee.
The lie that I told has come home to me.
'Oh no, dear husband, no boy did I see.'

Fee Fum Fi Fo.
'Help!' sang the golden harp, but oh,
The boy was quick and my husband slow.

Fo Fum Fee Fi.
I hear it still, that terrible cry.
No hen, no harp and no husband have I.

Cowlick

How
Can a cow
Stick its tongue up its nostril?
Why
Cannot I
Do it too?

I
Try and try
And I'll always feel cross till
I reach *my* nostril.
Moo!

Brain Boss

I've never seen you; we've never met.
I cannot hear or touch you, and yet
You're there in my head, a part of me,
Helping me touch and hear and see.

You wiggle my fingers and lift my feet
And open my mouth when I want to eat.
You make me happy and sad and cross.
There's no doubt about it – you're the boss.

You summon my laughter, send out my screams,
Think all my thoughts and dream all my dreams,
And I can't keep count of the number of times
You've given me rhythms and found me rhymes.

So I'm writing this poem, brain, for you –
Though I wonder now if that's really true.
The more I think, the more I see
That it's you who are writing the poem for me.

Question Time

How many books have you written?
Have you been writing for years?
Where do you get all the paper?
Where do you get your ideas?

Do you get bumps on your fingers?
Do you get aches in your wrist?
Please can I go to the toilet?
Did you write *Oliver Twist*?

I've got a book about spiders.
I've got a cut on my knee.
I've got an aunt who speaks German.
Gemma keeps tickling me.

Are you quite old? Are you famous?
Are you a millionaire?
I wasn't putting my hand up –
I was just twiddling my hair.

How many plays have you written?
Do you write one every day?
Do you . . . oh dear, I've forgotten
What I was going to say.

Will you be staying to dinner?
Will you go home on the bus?
How many poems have you written?
Will you write one about us?

Who's There?

Clink clink clink! Who's there outside the door?
Clink clink clink! I've heard that sound before.
It's the milkman leaving a bottle by your door.
You can pour some on your cereal or suck it through
 a straw.
You can give some to the cat, and watch her lap it up.
You can drink it from your favourite – clink clink –
 cup.

Clackety clack thump! Who's there outside the door?
Clackety clack thump! I've heard that sound before.
It's the postman's letters; they're falling on the mat.
There is one that's brown and boring. There's another
 nice and fat.
There's a postcard from a friend with a picture of the
 sea
And a lovely lumpy parcel for – clackety thump – me.

Bang clang clash! Who's there outside the door?
Bang clang clash! I've heard that sound before.
It's the dustman's clatter. He's emptying the bins,
All the bits and bobs and turnip tops, the tea leaves
 and the tins,
Into his noisy dusty cart that goes rumble rumble
 bump
As he drives it all the way to the – bang clash – dump.

72

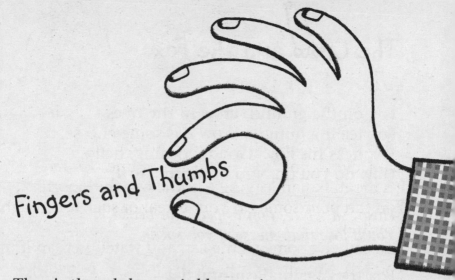

Fingers and Thumbs

Theo's thumb has wrinkles on it
Because he likes sucking it.
Tammy's tallest finger has a bump on the side
    of it
Because she likes writing.
Fred's fingertips have hard thick skin
Because he likes playing the guitar.
Aunt Edna's little finger curls in the air when
    she drinks tea
Because she likes to look elegant.
One of my great-grandmother's fingers has a
    thimble on it
Because she likes sewing.
Mum's ring finger has a ring on it
Because she likes Dad.
And my fingernails all have dirt under them
Because dirt likes me.

The Crow and the Fox

Fox on the ground, crow in the trees.
Fox feeling hungry, crow has some cheese.
Fox licks his lips. 'Good morning, hello.
How do you do, you beautiful crow?'

Hush, silly bird, don't open your beak –
You'll lose that cheese if you speak.

Fox tries again: 'Beautiful day,
Don't you agree? What do you say?
Elegant bird with feathers so sleek,
Can you be dumb? Why don't you speak?'

Hush, silly bird, don't open your beak –
You'll lose that cheese if you speak.

'Your wings and your tail are glossy and dark.
Your eyes are like diamonds, your voice like a lark.
Sing for me now! Oh how I long
To hear just one note – won't you sing me a
    song?'

Hush, silly bird, don't open your beak –
You'll lose that cheese if you speak.

Crow feeling good, puffing with pride,
Eyes shining brightly, head on one side.

Opens her beak, lets out a sound – CAAAAAAGH!
Down falls the cheese to fox on the ground.

Hush, silly bird, why did you croak?
You lost that cheese when you spoke.

Fox on the ground, crow in the trees,
Crow feeling hungry, fox has the cheese.

Come to the Library

Everyone is welcome to walk through the door.
It really doesn't matter if you're rich or poor.
There are books in boxes and books on shelves.
They're free for you to borrow, so help
    yourselves.

Come and meet your heroes, old and new,
From William the Conqueror to Winnie the
    Pooh.
You can look into the *Mirror* or read *The Times*,
Or bring along a toddler to chant some rhymes.

The librarian's a friend who loves to lend,
So see if there's a book that she can recommend.
Read that book, and if you're bitten
You can borrow all the other ones the author's
    written.

Are you into battles or biography?
Are you keen on gerbils or geography?
Gardening or ghosts? Sharks or science fiction?
There's something here for everyone, whatever
    your addiction.

There are students revising, deep in
    concentration,
And school kids doing projects, finding
    inspiration.
Over in the corner there's a table with seating,
So come along and join in the Book Club
    meeting.

Yes, come to the library! Browse and borrow,
And help make sure it'll still be here tomorrow.

One Tongue

One tongue, one lollipop.
Lick, lick, lick.
One tongue, no more lollipop.
Just one stick.

Two Feet

Two feet, out for a run.
Two shoes, with laces undone.
Bang! Crash! Two disasters.
Two knees with sticking plasters.

Three Bears

Three bears went out a-walking.
They left their table set.
They came back home, and Baby Bear
Began to cry and fret.
'Someone's had my porridge!
It was Goldilocks, I bet.'
His mum said, 'Don't be silly, dear –
I haven't cooked it yet.'

Four Strings

One between-knees, three under-chins:
Cello, viola and two violins.
Four chairs, four stands, four bows and four
    players
And a wonderful tune with four different layers.

Five Points

I saw a starfish, sitting on the sand.
It had five points, like the fingers on my hand.
I asked it the way, but the starfish didn't know.
It kept on pointing five ways to go.

Six Eggs

Six eggs – one to bake,
One to boil and one to break,
One for a pudding, one for a cake
And one to hatch into . . . A RATTLESNAKE!

Seven Sisters

The seven sisters stand by the sea.
They stand in a row in the salt sea air.
Crabs tickle their rocky toes,
Sheep nibble their grassy hair,
Birds nest in their chalky bodies,
But what do the seven sisters care?
When the crabs and the sheep and the
    birds have gone
The seven sisters will still be there.

The Seven Sisters are cliffs, part of the Sussex coast

Eight Tentacles

If only I had an octopus
I'd soon get my housework done.
I'd set him to work on the hoovering
With tentacle number one.
Tentacle two would grab a mop
And start on the kitchen floor
While he dusted and polished the furniture
With tentacles three and four.
Tentacle five would turn on the tap
And tackle the washing-up
While tentacle six took a well-earned break
And curled round a china cup.
Tentacle seven would make the beds
And set all the pillows straight,
And all the time he'd be balancing
On tentacle number eight.

Nine Nines

Here comes Vera Victoria Vines
Who always dresses up to the nines.

This is what Vera likes to wear:
Nine pink ribbons in her hair,
Nine gold bracelets round her arms
(Each one with nine lucky charms),
Beads around her neck (nine strings)
And on her fingers nine bright rings.
Nine silk hankies trimmed with lace,
Nine beauty spots upon her face,
A dress with nine pearl buttons on it
And nine bananas on her bonnet.

There goes Vera Victoria Vines
Dressed, as always, up to the nines.

Toe Number Ten

What shall I call my little left toe?
I've chosen good names for the others.
Joshua, Jeremy, John, James and Joe –
Those are the names of her brothers.
The names of her sisters are Stephanie-Joan,
Sophie, Samantha and Sue,
But my little left toe needs a name of her own
And I can't seem to find one. Can you?

Index of Poems

Index of First Lines

Julia Donaldson
Princess
Mirror-Belle

'I'm Princess Mirror-Belle. You really ought to curtsy, but as you're my friend I'll let you off.'

Ellen has a big surprise when she looks into her bathroom mirror – and sees a mysterious girl. It can't be her reflection because reflections don't talk back! The girl says her name is Mirror-Belle and that she's a princess from a magical faraway palace.

Soon Mirror-Belle and Ellen are friends. But Mirror-Belle is very naughty and she's about to lead Ellen into all kinds of amazing and exciting adventures...

Six delightfully funny stories from a much-loved and bestselling author

Julia Donaldson

A wicked wolf on the prowl

Two clever crooks in search of loot

A beautiful girl imprisoned in the underworld

From traditional to modern, from fantasy to fun, there's a part for everyone in this brilliant collection of eleven short plays written by bestselling author Julia Donaldson.

Perfect for primary school or family use, and suitable for a wide variety of ages and abilities, *Play Time* provides everything the budding actor needs to raise the curtain on the wonderful world of theatre!